AF431197

Can I have a kiss?

Pilar Gómez de Villalba

Title: Can I have a kiss?
Author: Pilar Gómez de Villalba
Images: Pilar Gómez de Villalba

*"Body and soul are not two
different things,
but only two different ways
of perceiving the same thing"*

Albert Einstein

Can I have a
kiss?

Can I have a
hug?

We kiss and
hug each
other, as
expression of
feelings of
love,
friendship and
affection.

If I ask you for
a kiss,
you should kiss
me because
you feel like
doing so...

You kiss me
because it
makes you feel
GOOD.

Kisses are not
required.

NO ONE has the
right to expect
them if YOU do
not want to.
And NOBODY
can force you to
accept one.

Kisses are not
negotiable.
They are not
exchanged for
gifts.

Because real kisses are given without asking for anything in return.

Even if one day
you go to play
without kissing
me, I know you
love me ... and
I love you too!

If one day you
don't feel like
hugging me (or a
friend) ...

It's OK.

We still love you
deeply.

Because real
kisses and
hugs are given
and received
when you feel
like it.

They are
given because
you feel you
want to, and
they are
accepted
because they
are desired.

YOU CHOOSE
when to give
them and
when to
receive them.

Real kisses
make us feel
amazing, and
they fill us with
happiness.

Similarly, the kisses and the hugs of your family members are wonderful! That's why ...

I love you
when you give
me a kiss, and I
will always
love you even
if you make
me wait for it.

The end.

Author's Note to Parents

As a child, I often observed my friends being scolded when they did not want to give a kiss as a greeting (to one of their parent's friends, a neighbour or a relative).

I always wondered why my friends were OBLIGED to show affection, and obliged to ACCEPT it in return!

When a child's freedom to choose when and how to express and receive love is not respected, it can affect their judgement of what is acceptable as an adult.

Since having children of my own and over time, I have endeavoured to study and inform myself about multiple issues related to childhood.

In 2010 I read a wonderful article titled "Los besos no se piden, los besos se regalan" (kisses are not required, you give them for free) in the Spanish magazine "Bebés y más" which I found highly instructive.

Such a basic idea, so simple, but nowadays so easily overlooked.

Children are like a beautiful ball full of love, but understandably, they show that love when they WANT TO.

And they are happy to receive affection if they WANT TO.

I think that forcing them, both to show or receive affection, is harmful.

Forcing them to kiss when they do not want to may cause them to become confused in the future, about whether they have in choosing to kiss or not to kiss.

Forcing them to receive a kiss, (a hug or any other sign of affection), can produce a similar effect.

An obligation of showing or accepting affection may be confusing when the time comes for children to be discerning about when they can say "NO", (which, of course, they need to ALWAYS know that they can say).

Our children are our most precious treasure, and raising them in the most respectful and caring way is a task that all of us want to succeed at.

It is for this reason that I have written this little book, so that our little ones can receive two clear messages:

"THEY HAVE THE POWER TO DECIDE."

"NO MEANS NO, BOTH IF YOU SAY IT AND IF YOU HEAR IT"

I have wanted to associate these messages with images that represent their meaning.

Therefore, for many months I have been painting and my three- and six-year old children have helped me by picking their favourite paintings), in order to include the images that are most representative and appealing to children.

I sincerely hope that you like this book.

Thank you for reading it.

Pilar Gómez de Villalba.

www.ingramcontent.com/pod-product-compliance
Lightning Source LLC
Chambersburg PA
CBHW040928110726
48006CB00001B/104